OLD WOOD ◆ NEW HOME

OLD WOOD  NEW HOME

G. Lawson Drinkard III

Photographs by Audrey Hall

GIBBS·SMITH
P
PUBLISHER

Salt Lake City

First Edition
05 04 03 02 01 00   5 4 3 2 1

Published by
Gibbs Smith, Publisher
P.O. Box 667
Layton, Utah 84041

Orders: (1-800) 748-5439
Web site: www.gibbs-smith.com

Designed and produced by Jeff Pollard
    Pollard & Van de Water, Boulder, Colorado
Printed and bound in Korea

Library of Congress Cataloging-in-Publication Data

Drinkard, G. Lawson, 1951–
   Old wood new home/G. Lawson Drinkard III ; photography by Audrey Hall.
   p.cm.
   ISBN 0-87905-953-2
   1.Log cabins—Design and construction. 2. Timber—Recycling. Title.
   TH4849 .D56 2000
   690'.873—dc21
                              00-035758

To my great-grandparents Frank and Julia Buch,
who, without ever knowing it,
blessed me by following their dream.

Contents

Acknowledgements   ix

Terry Baird, Artist Builder   x

Homestead Heritage   1

First Things First   7

Moving Your Treasure   20

Building Your Own Nest   28

Blending Old with New   47

House into Home   103

Resources   126

ACKNOWLEDGEMENTS

So many folks contributed to the undertaking of this book. Some were directly involved, some provided assistance, and others played unseen roles whose magnitude was greater than they might have understood.

Without the support, guidance, and gentle persistence of my editor, Madge Baird, this project wouldn't have been started or completed. Audrey Hall approached the photography with an artist's eye and unbounded enthusiasm. Jeff Pollard offered a fresh and spirited design approach. Terry and Jill Baird answered my countless questions and offered their wealth of experience. My Montana touchstones, Steve and Jeane Aller, allowed countless photographic sessions amidst planning for their daughter's wedding and always provided generous western hospitality.

So many were generous in allowing Audrey and me to intrude into their homes and their lives for photographs and questions. Thanks so much to Nan Newton and Dave Grusin, Lexi Rome, Michael Keaton, Hilary Heminway, Margot Jones, David Stanley and Jean Keffeler, and Dick and Sue Jacobsen.

And there are those friends who always offer the hidden hands of interest, love, inspiration, and succor. I couldn't have done it without you. Thanks to Marci and Chas, Ron and Trish, Jay and Beth, Dawna and Andy, Tina, Arch and Gwen, Jack, Mike, Carol, Don, and Dayton.

Finally, thanks to my mother, sister, daughter, and wife for your enduring love, nourishment, and tolerance.

G. Lawson Drinkard III

TERRY BAIRD, ARTIST BUILDER

The marvelous log homes created by master log reclaimer Terry Baird of McLeod, Montana, were the inspiration and resources for this book. His independent spirit and his artistic inner voice led Baird to look for something more interesting and challenging than building conventional houses. In Montana, he got involved with constructing and renovating homes, a fair number of which were made of logs. Though at first he had no log-building experience, he brought to his projects a trial-and-error spirit and was able to ask questions and learn from other log-home builders in the area as they gathered after work. The McLeod Bar was his classroom, and the construction site was his laboratory and studio.

Baird rapidly gained experience and a reputation for reclaiming and renovating elegant log cabins in southwest Montana. Because of his inquisitive approach, every job would lead to some new understanding of how to do things differently or better. On every project he would invent or refine some new concoction or method that helped him transform the aged into the new, but his work still retained the character and spirit of the old. He learned from his clients, his crew, and by making some mistakes. All of his experiences were filtered and filed away somewhere in his cerebrum, and over time these have become a part of his own personal style and philosophy of building. His approach involves salvaging and reclaiming old wood and transforming it into living spaces that have unique personalities.

He noticed that when most people built or renovated a log house, they tended to use materials they could get at the local lumberyard, such as aluminum-clad windows, shiny galvanized hardware, and metal-clad doors. Instead, he scrounges materials from dilapidated barns, junk piles, and old homestead sites. He has swapped for or bought hoary log buildings that may still wait in storage for years until he finds just the right use or new owner for them. This is Baird's personal approach to environmental sustainability, and at the same time it allows him and his clients to preserve small bits of homestead history.

Baird's unique style and high level of artistic craftsmanship have led to his being one of the most sought-after builders of homes and retreat places in Montana. Though the cabins in this book depict a wide variety of styles, sizes, and users, they all have one thing in common: each represents the elegant craftsmanship, keen vision, and artistic ability of one man. Of course, Baird is not the only builder who specializes in reclaiming old buildings and recycling them into new homes, but he is one of the best in America at his craft.

XI

*Baird traded some construction services for a homestead
cabin, moved it to this site from fifty miles away,
and with his wife, Jill, built a rustic retreat.*

HOMESTEAD HERITAGE

In an era entranced by "the new" our greatest hope ironically may lie in the rediscovery of "the old."

— Peter Senge, from *Leading Consciously* by Degashis Chatterjee
Butterworth-Heinemann, 1998

Sometime in 1908 my great-grandparents Frank and Julia Buch, along with three small children aged eleven, nine, and five, made their way from Bentonville, Arkansas, to claim a homestead near the newly formed town of Powell, Wyoming. There they found a desert covered with sagebrush and cactus, but they followed the promise of a lush and fertile valley that would be irrigated as a result of the Shoshone Reclamation Project and the building of the Shoshone Dam, what we now know as the Buffalo Bill Dam. Though the land was harsh and unforgiving, they built a small house and pasture fence, and they helped to build the Union Presbyterian Church. They endured the hardships of tornadoes, blizzards, and drought, but they survived and prospered and set before me the example of following one's dream. And they created for me a genetic connection to the West and an abiding interest in the subject of this book.

The seemingly insatiable desire of humans to push the geographic boundaries of the earth has for centuries led women and men to journey into uncharted lands. As the United States was resettled by migrating Europeans, those early conquerors of the North American continent built simple shelters as they migrated west. These buildings were constructed of readily available materials and were built by hand with limited labor and technology. Some were built of sod, some of canvas, some of stone, and many of wood. The pioneer log cabin has become as much a symbol of westward movement as the oxen or the covered wagon.

2

Above and right:
Modeled after a building type prevalent in early mining boomtowns, this canvas
wall tent designed and built by Hilary Heminway and Terry Baird is a one-room
retreat made of old boards and recycled pine poles. The sheer netting over the bed
gives these sleeping quarters all the romance of an African safari camp.

4

As you contemplate

each planning decision,

ask yourself "What

can I do here that will

make my heart sing?"

An outdoor setup for meal preparation brings the
homestead spirit to a contemporary lifestyle.

The Homestead Act of 1862 promised 160 acres of free public land to anyone who would build a house, dig a well, build a fence, and farm at least 10 acres—and do it for at least five years. By 1900, 600,000 people had taken advantage, claiming more than 80 million acres. Dotted from ocean to ocean across the landscape of America are remnants of these family homes, barns, and sheds from an earlier time. Some are falling down and are barely recognizable. Some have already been pushed into a pile and burned to make way for subdivisions, barns, or strip shopping malls. And, thankfully, many are still standing and retain some useful life.

Though there are some similarities between today's modern log homes and settlers' cabins of the past, there are also significant differences. Most present-day log homes are built entirely of new materials—tree-farm-grown logs, carpeted floors, pre-finished doors, thermal-pane windows, and the like. They are electrified, have indoor plumbing, and are usually heated by a central system rather than a fireplace.

The projects and people you will find in the following pages demonstrate a different way of approaching the process of building shelter and of how one chooses to live. For sure, most of these homes are not without telephones, indoor plumbing, or the ability for their owners to surf the Web, but they all represent an unconventional approach to home building that is more about the journey than it is about how fast the project is completed. They are all made, at least partially, with materials reclaimed from another use in an earlier time. They have all been put together with creativity, love, and painstaking care. They have all taken extra time to build—time to find, reclaim, restore, and reuse old things, sometimes in new and different ways than they were originally intended. They all demanded patience and a tolerance for the uncertain and unknown. They all presented surprises for the owners and builders—some fortunate and some less so. They all have paid at least some debt of gratitude and recognition to Mother Nature by reusing natural resources that had previously been harvested. They each have a unique personality and spirit that can never be reproduced or copied anywhere by anyone. And they are all joyous places to live, work, and play.

Whether you are contemplating building your own home from reclaimed parts or just dreaming for the future, I invite you to immerse yourself in the surprising possibilities of transforming the old into the new.

5

FIRST THINGS FIRST

Though you have never actually taken the time for a closer inspection, you have driven by that enchanting barn or old log cabin for years. As you motor past, you just cannot resist slowing ever so slightly to take a longing peek. For a very long time you've had a secret desire to make it your own: to collect it like a piece of antique art, or to take it home and give it a new life. Your inner voice is whispering, "Stop, please stop and look," but the larboard side of your brain is shouting, "I don't have time today, and besides, I'd never have the skills or the talent to make it come alive again." Someday (hopefully soon) your heart might win the tussle with your head. You won't be able to resist that ancient genetic code that draws us to hearth and home like a red-tailed hawk headed south in the fall.

There is no harm in a quick look, right? However, what if that first date attracts you to consider a longer relationship?

More questions arise, such as:

- *What might I use such a cabin for?*

- *Where could I put it?*

- *What kind of shape is it in?*

- *How should I approach the owner about a purchase?*

- *How much might it cost?*

USES FOR OLD LOG STRUCTURES

There are at least two approaches to this question. One assumes you have acquired (or want to acquire) an old log structure and wish to find a reason to reclaim it. Another presumes that you already have a use in mind and are searching for just the right structure (or structures) to enable you to accomplish your plan. For the purposes of exercising our imaginations, let's look at the question "I've got an old log cabin; what might I do with it?"

The answer is, whatever you want! Anything you can imagine can be accommodated in a reclaimed log building or a combination of buildings. The choices that come to mind most readily are a permanent home, a summer cabin, or a small guest cottage. Here is a list of some other potential uses. What new ones can you add to it? What can you dream about that you'd like to do or have in an old log building?

- *Playhouse*
- *Gardening Shed*
- *Wood Shop*
- *Art Gallery*
- *Pottery Studio*
- *Office*
- *Music Room*
- *Poet's Corner*
- *Bunkhouse*
- *Tack Room*
- *Painting Studio*
- *Bread Kitchen*
- *Napping Room*
- *Quilting Studio*

- *Honeymoon Cottage*
- *Garage*
- *Antiques Store*
- *Fly-Tying Studio*
- *Hunting Cabin*
- *In-law Quarters*
- *Sauna*
- *Blacksmith Shop*
- *Library*
- *Pet Motel*
- *Centerpiece for a Larger Structure (with add-ons)*

A comfortable guest bunkhouse results from the
creative reconstitution of a chicken coop.

Places to Put Your Structure

Naturally, if you purchase an old log or timber structure, you'll want to have a place to relocate it for its new use. Whether you intend to put your new building on property you already own or to purchase a new piece of land, you'll want to consider issues like zoning and building codes, views, topography, natural characteristics, and site orientation. It is a good idea to spend considerable time on a piece of property before deciding to locate a building there. Get to know the land, how it feels, how it flows, what it says to you when you wake up in the morning and when you close your eyes at night.

Here is a checklist of things to think about as you consider siting your relocated building. This isn't a definitive list but rather one to get you started and to raise more questions.

Zoning and Legal Issues

- *Is the property zoned? If so, how?*
- *What zoning restrictions exist for this specific piece of property?*
- *Is there a local building code and does it apply?*
- *Are there any deed restrictions?*
- *What are the yearly taxes?*
- *Is the property in the floodplain or a wetlands area?*
- *Are there deeded riparian rights or mineral rights?*
- *Are the property lines correctly defined?*
- *Is a title search necessary?*

Natural Characteristics

- *What is the direction of prevailing winds or breezes?*
- *What are the views from your cabin—long-range, mid-range, short-range?*
- *Can you see your neighbors? Do you want to?*
- *What will be the views of your cabin from adjacent properties?*
- *How does the sunlight move across the property in each season?*
- *What is the topography and slope of the property?*
- *Are there trees and natural formations that need to be considered?*
- *Is there evidence of subsurface stone?*
- *Does the site drain properly?*
- *Where will the road or driveway go, and what will be the necessary grades?*
- *Can building materials be delivered economically?*

Utilities

- *Is electricity available?*
- *Is telephone service available?*
- *Is natural or bottled gas available?*
- *Is "city" water available?*
- *Is there a potable water source?*
- *What is the local success rate for drilling, digging, or boring a well?*
- *Does the soil percolate?*
- *Is sewage disposal available?*

Nan Newton's studio sited to nestle between towering trees.

Above and right:
Nan Newton's one-room office/studio is constructed of wood
frame and covered on the exterior with log slabs. The interior is
finished with rough-sawn boards on the floor, walls, and ceiling.

EVALUATING YOUR STRUCTURE

This is a place where some trained eyes and experience might be helpful. You will be able to detect potential problems that are visually obvious, such as logs that are rotted on the outside. Many logs rot from the outside in, but some logs (for instance, oak and chestnut) can rot from the inside out as a result of water seeping into small chinks and cracks. Sticking a knife blade or a nail into suspect timbers will give you a clue as to their soundness.

There are also a variety of critters that may have done damage to the wood over time. Termites and powder-post beetles may have infested the structure, and building with logs that have been damaged by these insects—or worse, are still infested with them—will cause problems for you down the road.

As a rule of thumb, if a cabin or old barn has been sitting for many years without the benefit of a roof to protect it from the elements, it is likely that much of the structure will be useless. No matter what your emotional or romantic attachment may be to an old cabin, make sure there are enough useable materials to make a purchase and relocation worth your while.

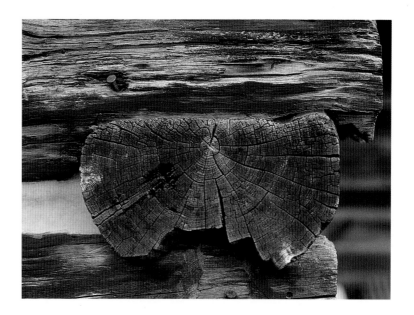

15

Though the end of this log shows some deterioration, it was still solid enough to be used again in this restacked cabin.

Left:
Depending on how long this old barn has been without a roof, the logs may or may not still have useful life. They should be inspected carefully for rot, termites, and other wood-eating critters before they are scheduled for use on a new structure. Even if the logs are not useful, the building may hold artifacts that could add interest and character to your project.

BUYING AN OLD LOG CABIN

There are no hard-and-fast rules about how to find, how to buy, and how much to pay for an old log building. Every situation will be unique. Consider that part of the adventure and the fun.

Finding a Cabin

The best way to find old structures is to get out into the country-side and look for them. Once your eyes and mind are tuned to look, you'll be surprised at how many are still standing in rural areas. Stop by a country store (if you can still find one that hasn't been converted into a convenience store) and talk with the proprietor. Ask around at the local feed store or agriculture equipment dealership. Especially in small towns, these folks know everyone who works the land in their local area.

Search old newspaper records, especially small-town weekly ones. There may have been an article about an old homestead cabin. The owner/publisher/editor can also be a good source of information. Placing an ad in country newspapers can also bring results, but it may serve to raise the potential purchase price by notifying the owners that they have something of value.

There are people who buy and dismantle old log buildings and offer them for sale. You can search the Internet or restoration and renovation magazines and newsletters for their advertisements.

Establishing Value

Ultimately, the value of anything is what you or someone else is willing to pay for it. How do you decide what an old cabin is worth to you? One way is to take the measurements or a sketch of the perimeter of the building to a reputable log-home-kit company and see what a new structure of the same size would cost. Some kits contain just the perimeter logs; some include rafters, roof, etcetera. Make sure you are comparing apples to apples, but don't try to be too scientific about it. You are just trying to see what a similar structure might cost if you bought it new. Another way is to try to figure out what it would cost to build the same amount of raw, unfinished space in frame construction. A local lumberyard might be helpful here, or a residential general contractor may be able to provide you with some building-cost data.

One rule of thumb is that almost any building is worth at least a thousand dollars. Depending on size, it could be worth a lot more. You should also consider what else you might be able to salvage other than the logs. Is there a good fir floor that can be reused for furniture or kitchen cabinets? Are there doors that can be refinished and hung again? Is there old tin on the roof that can be used as roofing material or siding? The package is what you will be buying, so you have to decide what the package is worth to you. Always remember the axiom of antiques dealers—they buy junk and sell antiques!

This old barn, with its roof still intact, promises to provide solid logs as raw material for a reborn building.

BUYING APPROACHES

If you know the owners well or are somehow related to them, direct conversation about a potential sale might work all right. But, if you are a stranger looking at cabins in a different county, you may want to try a softer approach. Generally speaking, old cabins are located in small towns or out in the country where most everyone knows everyone else (and their business!). You might stop at a local grocery store, a restaurant, or a bar and strike up a conversation. "Say, do you know who owns that old cabin out past the cemetery on Mission Creek Road?" One method that works well is to offer a finder's fee. "If you find out that cabin is for sale, I'll give you a hundred bucks." Once the ice is broken with the owner, it will be easier for you to come in and complete the deal.

You should always be trying to create value for the owner. Offer a little more for the cabin than you think the owner considers it to be worth. Remember how much you'll be saving in comparison to building the same amount of space with new materials. If they haven't done anything with their building in the last twenty years, they might be interested in tearing it down and cleaning up the mess in order to create a little more pasture or get it off the tax rolls. Promise to come in, disassemble or move the cabin, and pile all of the trash neatly so it can be hauled away or burned in the dead of winter.

Many old cabins have other relics hanging around inside or outside that can be used on your new project, but don't just assume they come with the deal. Make sure that you have agreement with the owner as to exactly what you are buying. Old lanterns, bathtubs, light fixtures, horse troughs, barrels, washtubs, boxes, and beds can all be used in creative ways to construct or decorate a reclaimed cabin.

Finding and buying an old log structure is a bit like a scavenger hunt with a little Sherlock Holmes thrown in. Part of the fun is in finding and purchasing someone else's junk that you have the vision to turn into your own personal treasure.

MOVING YOUR TREASURE

You have found and purchased your log cabin, barn, or spring-house and are probably anxious to move it to the site you have selected. Your choices are to take your building apart and move it in pieces or to move it in its entirety. Your decision will depend on the size of the building, your budget, the amount of time you have, and available labor. Disassembly and moving in parts can be a do-it-yourself project, but moving an entire building will almost certainly require the assistance of a professional house mover.

PRELIMINARY STEPS

No matter which transit choice you make, there are some steps you should take before you start to move anything. Documenting your building and making it safe to work around will save you time and trouble in the long run.

For your scrapbook, take a few "before" photos of the building in its original state—trash and all. After your project is complete, you'll want these to show your disbelieving friends and family. They will also be handy when your local newspaper wants to do a story about the amazing new structure that you made from all of those old parts.

Take the time to clean in and around your building. Remember that safety is of paramount importance here. Wear eye protection, sturdy shoes, a hard hat, and heavy gloves, and make sure your tetanus shot is up to date. Broken glass, rotting timbers, and rusty nails all represent potential accidents. Make sure the electricity is off before you touch any wiring. Stay alert and use good common sense.

Depending on the location and period of construction, it is possible that plaster, insulation, or window glazing may contain asbestos. If you have any reason to suspect its presence, the material will need to be inspected and removed by a certified specialist before you disturb it in any way. It is also possible that wood trim inside or outside the structure may have been painted with a lead-based paint. Sanding or disturbing this paint can be hazardous, so it must be handled with proper precautions. If you have any questions about the possibility of asbestos or lead-based paint, consult your local building official for further information and assistance.

In many areas of the country, hantavirus has become more prevalent, so you may want to take some special precautions if there have been mice (evidenced by mouse droppings) in the structure. Wearing a dust mask and gloves and spraying all surfaces with a light mixture of bleach and water before raising lots of dust are good precautionary measures. If you have any concerns about this issue, consult the health department before you begin to sweep.

Start a burn pile outside if it is allowed, or lease a dumpster for the debris you will remove. Clean up all of the trash, rotten wood, old shingles, and rubbish in and around the building. Take care not to throw away any "junk" that could be reused as treasure in your new building. Old brackets, hinges, rusty nails, and scraps of tin can all come in handy later.

After your building has been cleaned up, take the time to document it thoroughly before starting to take it down or alter it in any way. If you intend to put the parts back together the way they came apart, measure and draw a rough floor plan of the existing conditions. Film is cheap. Take plenty of photographs from all possible angles. If you have a video camera, film might come in handy later as well. If you have a digital camera and some sort of photo-manipulation software for your computer, electronic images can be used to study potential design solutions, colors, materials, and so on.

This rustic structure was once a log motel miles from its present site. It was moved intact and added onto after relocation.

TAKING IT DOWN

If you intend to take your cabin apart to move it, the logs will need to be carefully numbered before they are pulled apart. Start at one corner and designate it corner "A." From the bottom, number your logs 1A, 2A, 3A, and so forth until you get to the top log. Make sure the labels you use are sturdy; staple them tightly to the ends of the logs. Be sure to use a waterproof ink if the logs are to be stacked outdoors. It is a good idea to mark each log several times, inside and outside, in case one of the labels gets pulled off. Go to the next corner and designate it corner "B." Starting at the bottom, number to the top again. Repeat this labeling method for every corner and log intersection in the building.

After you have finished labeling, take more photographs of the corners with the labels attached. These will be invaluable when you start to reassemble the building. Draw a map of the building and the labeling system you used. Don't trust your memory. If you do, you may regret it later when you just can't figure out how things should fit back together.

The size of your old cabin and its location will determine what tools and equipment you need to take it apart. If it is located on a remote site, you will probably need a portable 30KW power generator and heavy-duty power cords. A contractor-grade reciprocating saw will allow you to cut through old bolts and spikes before you pry the logs apart. You will need a supply of various-sized pry bars and wrecking bars to take things apart. Pry

the logs apart just enough to allow you to cut through the fastener. Make sure not to leave crowbar "tracks" on the logs as you lever them apart. After you loosen each log, roll it off and onto a set of waiting sawhorses. Take the time to use a punch and remove the spikes or bolts. Take the nails out as you go and have a bucket handy to save them for later projects.

As you remove the logs, stack them in order with matching ends so your reassembly job will be easier. Depending on size, they may be moved in a pickup truck, or perhaps you will need a flatbed trailer.

If the cabin has a wooden floor, salvage as much of it as you can. Though you may not want to reuse the wood as flooring, it can come in handy for future cabinets, furniture, or paneling. Sometimes it is easier to remove if you first saw it into eight-foot lengths before you pry it up. Again, take the time to remove all the nails and fasteners before you stack it to be moved.

When the pieces of your cabin are delivered to the new site, they should be stacked in an orderly fashion and placed on pallets or old logs to keep them from contact with the ground. If they are going to be reassembled in short order, they probably don't need protection from the weather, but if it is going to be some time before construction begins, they should be covered.

Handsomely crafted
dovetail logs like these
could be numbered,
disassembled, moved,
then restacked to look as
beautiful as they do here.

MOVING IT WHOLE

Taking down a log building and restacking it somewhere else takes a lot of time, patience, and elbow grease. If you plan to do all of the work yourself, this is probably your only choice.

If, however, you plan on contracting out the move, it may be less expensive and save some time if you move the structure in its entirety. The practicality and expense of moving an intact structure will depend on its size, the distance you want to move it, and the obstacles likely to be encountered along the way. Narrow bridges, gates, city streets, and low-hanging electric and telephone lines are a few of the possible impediments a house mover may face. One of the first things you should do is explore the possible routes of travel between the original location and your new site. A professional house mover can give you an estimate as to the likely cost of moving your structure. If such a company is not listed in your local yellow pages, try contacting several reputable general contractors for names—especially contractors who specialize in renovation work. The approach to the move and the foundation work will be different for each building and each site.

Whether you move your cabin in pieces or as a whole, the exciting work begins when you get it to your new site and begin the task of reclaiming the old structure and turning it into your new dream. Now the real fun begins!

BUILDING YOUR OWN NEST

There was no standard design for pioneer and homestead cabins. Independent spirits, handiness of raw materials, intended use, geography, time available for construction, and the availability of help while the cabins were being erected determined their sizes and shapes. Thus, the building you have found and are reclaiming is almost certainly a unique structure. It was that way when finished by the original owner, and in the same wonderful way it will be a one-of-a-kind home when you finish giving it new life.

Whether your cabin is large or small, contains one or two multiuse spaces, or has a multitude of rooms, it will likely have a combination of elements that include living space, kitchen space, bathroom space, and sleeping space. Depending on its size, your construction budget, location, available utilities, and intended use, these functions can all occur within a single structure, or some can take place outdoors or in separate buildings.

No matter what the size, shape, or new use of your building, you will want to make it functional and comfortable as well as a reflection of your personal style. For design assistance, you may want to employ the services of a professional architect or an interior designer who specializes in restoration, renovation, and reclamation of old buildings. Log buildings present special challenges for designers, so be careful in your choice. Make sure the professionals you hire have the experience, attitude, or aptitude to work with this unique—and sometimes confounding—building type. An appealing alternative is to strike out on your own into unknown territory, like the early American pioneers did. This path will come with its own set of challenges, lessons, and surprises.

Not only does the owner of this house love to display cherished pieces of art, but the clerestory windows are framed to mimic paintings as well.

This low-stone structure was sited in response to the view, and to the constant wind that blows in the winter months.

In either case, a good way to start is by collecting as many books, magazines, and photographs as you can that will help you and others see potential solutions to the various design opportunities presented by your specific building. It is a good idea to mark the books and save the articles in folders by categories—kitchens, bathrooms, bedrooms, porches, window treatments, etcetera. This will add a little discipline to your research and make the material easier for you or someone else to use later. You will have to be careful as you search; many of the photographs you find will be of large, lavish new designs created with materials fresh from the lumberyard and furnishings straight from the showroom or reproduction shop. With a little practice (and after studying the photographs in this book), you will begin to be able to pick out materials, furnishings, and accessories that—living a second or third life—will add the kind of warmth and charm to your project that store-bought pieces can't match. Once you begin to train your mind and eyes to scan materials and objects in a different way, you will be surprised at the design ideas that will pop up all around you.

At a minimum, your cabin should be functional and serve its intended purpose. Bedrooms need to have places to sleep and to store clothes, bathrooms need the requisite fixtures, and kitchens need the appropriate appliances arranged in functional working relationships to each other. This may sound quite obvious, but I installed a combination washer/dryer in my small cabin kitchen only to find out that we couldn't fully open the refrigerator door—so we can't use the vegetable bins! In fact, many homestead cabins never went beyond the rather narrow criteria of shelter from the elements. A dry roof overhead with the means to keep one warm in the winter and to prevent one from baking in the summer set the design tone. Having to build with a limited vocabulary of materials and creating a space that was easy to heat usually meant a low-ceilinged structure with one exterior door and few, if any, windows. Cabins were sited as a response to the elements, not to the view. As Teresa Jordan so aptly described in her Wyoming chronicle *Riding the White Horse Home,* "The house I grew up in was built into the hill for insulation and shelter from the wind; the barn, too, was built into the hill so that hay could be unloaded directly into its loft. The design of each building, each corral, each ditch, was tied directly to the creative act of staying alive."

Since you are probably building your cabin for the pleasure of living or vacationing rather than for the bare necessity of shelter, a different set of design parameters will drive your planning decisions. Surely you will want all the rooms and spaces to accommodate their basic functions—but, after that, you'll want these places to ring with spirit, surprise, beauty, personality, and joy. As you contemplate each planning or decorating decision, ask yourself this simple question: What can I do here that will make my heart sing?

There are myriad ways to think about personalizing your own cabin. Let's look at a few.

ROOMS WITH A VIEW

Windows and doors can be placed, or buildings can be situated, to visually capture and frame what's important to you. A short-range view of a garden, a rock arrangement, or a flowering tree can become your own series of natural "paintings." A long-range vista of your private cove, or a frame for the rising sun from your favorite contemplative chair, can turn an ordinary room into a personal sanctuary.

A long-range view of the western slope of the Grand Tetons is framed perfectly by the doors and windows.

The nature scene out this window is a personal, private treasure.
No one else in the world sees it in quite the same way.

Glimpses from Your Past

Nothing seems more appropriate to the spirit of a homestead cabin than memorabilia that ties us, heart and soul, to our own heritage. Furniture, tools, or artifacts from past generations can be used in a variety of ways to add texture, interest, and an appreciation of the past into our spaces. In my own retreat cabin, I have hung on the wall by my favorite reading chair a set of cobbler tools used in Germany by my great-grandfather Buch to build and repair shoes. An old wooden chest that belonged to my great-aunt Annie made its way from Eureka, Missouri, to Lynchburg, Virginia, as a gift to my parents when they were married in 1950. Now it serves as a coffee table and a place to store linens in our Montana cabin. A simple cane rocker that belonged to my great-grandmother on the other side of my family helps me dream new dreams and rock away the clutter that clogs my mental arteries. A friend in Cody, Wyoming, has covered an entire living room wall with a genealogical chart of her family tree that is made up of photographs of each member of the clan. To friends and acquaintances they are interesting, but to her they offer an important mooring to her past.

Every family history is different, but one thing we share is that we all have one. Finding some way to connect to your own offers rich possibilities for personalizing your own cabin.

If only it could speak, a vintage trunk could tell stories about journeys made, the belongings it carried, and the people it supported along the way.

34

An old-fashioned desk anchors the mood
of this room to generations past.

Simple Pleasures

For some, order and a sense of calm repose can best be obtained through disciplined simplicity. We can look to examples set by the Shakers or the Benedictine communities to see this quality at its best. Carefully choosing just a few pieces of furniture and art for a room can give it a sense of focus and peacefulness—an ideal setting to divert one's attention from the everyday clutter.

Though this tiny dormer space is hardly tall enough to stand in, it has been made into a nesting spot to be enjoyed with a warm drink.

No matter what the use of your building, it should be functional, comfortable, and a reflection of your own personal style.

Curious Collections

Is there anyone who doesn't collect something? Either grouped together or creatively displayed throughout a home, curious collections can give a dwelling personal spirit. One Montana friend decorated her small guest bathroom with a sizable collection of rabbits. Every available perch hosts a stuffed rabbit of one sort or another. If rabbits weren't such amicable creatures, it might be a bit scary to go in there. Another neighbor has carried a moose theme throughout his entire house—inside and out. Selecting a thank-you gift for this owner is a cinch.

Cabin spaces can be marvelous places for displaying art collections. Rather than pictures filling some empty wall spaces here and there, entire walls can be filled to the rafters with art of various shapes and sizes.

A collection of antlers brings personality to the log exterior.

Left:
An overstuffed modern couch not only provides a
nice contrast to the natural wood and old logs
but also helps to brighten the space.

Favorite quotes embellish decorative throw pillows done in a simple fabric.

Find/Restore/Reclaim/Recycle

Before making a major furniture-showroom expedition and spending a small fortune on just the right decorator pieces, consider some alternatives to shaping and warming your reclaimed environment. Take a look around your attic, barn loft, garage, basement, grandma's house, or local trash dumps with the idea of seeing fresh possibilities instead of rubbish. Challenge your creativity by imagining a whole range of new uses for any particular "find." After the first few predictable answers emerge, allow your imagination to take flight. Let your junk pile be your palette and your cabin a freshly stretched canvas. Half of the fun is in the painting. If you don't like the end result, turn the paper over and paint something else on the other side. In my own cabin, an old ham boiler serves as a magazine rack, a calf-weaning bucket with the original nipple is a desk wastebasket, and a wicker fishing creel holds pens, pencils, rubber bands and notepaper on the wall next to the telephone. Each vintage piece serves a new function while anchoring and delighting me with its old one—two for one!

Combing yard sales and flea markets for just the right piece of furniture at the right price (translation—not costing a fortune) can be an entertaining way to decorate a cabin so that it will fit your budget and be filled with your own personal treasures. Finding real bargains isn't as easy as it used to be, but having persistence and a keen eye will pay off.

*A richly decorated Victorian door
makes this front entrance sing.*

All of these furnishings were collected from flea markets, junk shops, and antiques stores.

*Handmade furniture and revitalized junk-store treasures
make this living area comfortable and personal.*

Build Your Own

Given the fact that you've been bold enough to take on a reclamation project in the first place, perhaps it's a good time to teach yourself to build furniture. One friend in Bozeman, Montana, decided a number of years ago that making furniture from sticks was a good way to earn enough money to feed her kids while being a stay-at-home mom. Now this woman is an acclaimed custom-furniture maker. She taught herself—and so can you. No need to go to your local big-box hardware super-market and equip yourself with a Romanoff's fortune worth of fancy power equipment. A hammer, saw, screwdriver, and drill, along with some materials you can pick up in your garage or the woods behind your house, are enough to start. Let the tools and materials talk to you; let your hands get the feel of them. Don't worry so much about the product as the process. Allow yourself the luxury of being surprised.

These are just a few ways to think about how you might person-alize your building and turn it into something that reflects who you are and how you want to live. Of course, there are many others. Part of the joy of reclaiming an old building is finding your own way to breathe new life into the spaces you create. Enjoy the journey!

The handcrafted headboard becomes a piece of cowboy art.

44

A pine-pole table, made by Jeane Aller, is a perfect complement to the materials and character of this space.

One-room cabins work well for uses like studios, offices, or napping parlors, but to accommodate more people or activities, additional rooms may be beneficial. Since most aging cabins are fairly small, there is a good chance that you will increase available space in some fashion. Gaining more room can be accomplished in a couple of basic ways: add on to the building you have, or add an additional small building or two to your collection.

Multiple Buildings

Though having an enclave of outbuildings is less convenient when it is dark or raining, grouping small buildings together in a pleasing arrangement can be an attractive way to acquire additional space. Depending on the activity you have in mind, it can be entirely acceptable—and sometimes even desirable—to go outside and walk a short distance to another building. In earlier times, the kitchen was frequently in a separate structure, as was the barn, the smokehouse, the icehouse, and, of course, the privy. Rain or shine, light or dark, cold or warm, folks walked.

47

The logs and wood in these two renovated settlers' cabins were purchased for less than $5,000. The smaller of the two was the original homestead cabin and was later turned into an icehouse.

48

As my wife and I began to spend more and more time in our tiny (534-square-foot) cabin in Montana, it became necessary for me to create a place to do my daily support-the-family work. I needed a small office/studio from which to make a living. Since our retreat already had several small additions—a bedroom, a bathroom, a kitchen, and a porch—there was not an easy or practical way to add on without major disruption and expense. Instead, I decided to begin a "village" of small, unconnected structures arranged in a way that allows safe and convenient travel among them and that creates interesting exterior spaces by their juxtaposition to each other. After searching around a bit, I discovered a one-room log building with a fallen-in roof in a small town about fifty miles away. A small crew of people disassembled the old cabin in a morning, then loaded the logs onto several pickup trucks and had them back at my place by early afternoon. Over the winter, a foundation was built, the logs were restacked, and a new roof and a wraparound porch were added. Over several summers, the logs were re-chinked, electricity was added, and window screens were built—the old cabin has taken on a new life as my summer office and studio.

At present, the collection of buildings numbers three, including the main cabin, the office/studio, and a woodshed. The village is designed to grow.

Above and right:
This collection of old buildings was renovated exactly where
they were built in the 1920s. Originally a barn, a chicken
coop, and several cabins, they now house a guest cottage, an
owner's cabin, and a combination barn/efficiency apartment.
The old chicken coop was turned into a bunkhouse.

The interior of this cabin is finished and furnished simply. The floors, made of rough-sawn fir that has not been sanded, will be worn smooth over time.

Adding On

A more common way to gain additional space is to add it to the cabin you are reclaiming. Approaches can include blending two or three cabins together, adding a second story, cutting dormers into a roof, or adding small saddlebags to the sides of your cabin. What, how, and how much you add will directly correlate with the activities you want to accommodate and the opportunities the building itself affords. If you haven't already done it, now is probably a good time to draw a floor plan of your existing building and the additions you have in mind. The drawing doesn't have to be fancy, but you'll want to figure out how much space you need, how the rooms should relate to each other, and how such additions might work with your existing structure. For some, a small cardboard model is a helpful tool for visualizing what things might look like as you make your additions. A little time spent at this point can prevent mistakes, disappointment, lost time, and additional expense later on.

The wraparound porch is a grand addition of usable space to a building that would otherwise seem very small.

The Aller Residence

Because of other homes they had liked, Steve and Jeane Aller knew they wanted to build a log home from a reclaimed building. After an exhaustive search and rejecting a number of structures, they finally decided that the core of their new home should be constructed from a log stall barn that had been built on their ranch by miners at the turn of the twentieth century. It was a massive edifice, with some of the logs being as large as fourteen or fifteen inches in diameter; but, even at that, the Allers knew from the outset that it wouldn't—on its own—be big enough for their family of children and pets.

After making a number of rough sketches and even rougher cardboard models, they decided that the old barn would become the center of the house and would contain the living and dining areas on the main floor and a large bedroom on the second floor. That presented the challenge of adding areas for a kitchen, laundry room, master bedroom, master bathroom, sewing room, den, and office. These areas would require more space than the full measurement of the original barn. The task, then, was to make an addition that would respect and blend with the barn while not overshadowing the beautiful old construction with the new.

The logs were moved and restacked, carefully sited for protection from the winter wind and to feature the older part of the house as the main entry. The two-story addition was tucked to the side and rear of the building so as not to compete with the rich character of the old barn. A long front porch helped to couple the two parts of the structure and soften the connection.

The construction system the Allers chose for the addition was not stacked full logs but, rather, wood framing clad with log slabs on the outside and finished with rough-sawn wood or plaster on the inside. The exterior slabs give the appearance of full-log construction; they were treated with a liquid concoction that made their color match the color of the old barn logs almost perfectly. The slabs are screwed onto 5/8-inch plywood sheathing and chinked just like regular log construction.

When asked her advice about building such a house, Jeane Aller offered, "We went slowly so we could do what we wanted, and we didn't have to make quick decisions. You cannot move fast if you are fully involved in building the project yourself. Now that we are done, we know that we are really part of the house."

54

This light-filled sewing room is part of the newly added space in the Aller residence. The exterior is covered with log slabs and the interior is finished with whitewashed fir boards.

The upper floor of the barn structure was made into a generously sized bedroom. Dormers were added for light and to increase the ceiling heights.

The main floor area of this old barn has been transformed into the Allers' living room.

The Baird Residence

When Terry and Jill Baird first saw their cabin on the East Boulder River near McLeod, Montana, it was painted orange. The former owners, in trying to "modernize" it, had applied cheap wood paneling and ceiling tile, and had scattered floor tile all over the inside. The Bairds removed all of the various wall, floor, and ceiling coverings and discovered splendid logs and hard, vertical-grain fir floors. When they did their interior excavation and got back to the original walls, they found that many of the logs had been grooved, cut, and notched for electricity, plumbing, etcetera. To correct this damage and to bring some uniformity to the logs, they performed a bit of cosmetic surgery: with broadaxes they hewed the logs from round to flat and ended up with relatively consistent wall surfaces that had all the character of hundred-year-old wood.

Terry Baird refers to his home as "collective architecture." "It started out as a sixteen-by-twenty homestead cabin built in the 1890s," said Baird. "The story goes that they raised thirteen kids here. Then someone else lived here and added on another little cabin, somebody else added on a bedroom, and somebody else added a bathroom and a little wing." When the Bairds moved in, they added a kitchen, another bathroom, a TV room, and a bedroom on a second floor for their daughter. Every room is relatively small, each having its own function, but they flow together so that every space gains something from the adjacent spaces. Since the house is deep in a valley, the TV room/bedroom addition is wrapped in windows that capture the maximum sunlight and serve as a light funnel for the rest of the linear floor plan.

Approximately 50 percent of the existing structure is log construction and the other half is wood-frame construction with log slabs used as an outside finish material to maintain continuity. When you see it from the road, it's not a mishmash of different materials. The windows in the additions are similar to the existing ones, and on the interior, all of the wood trim matches from space to space, helping to tie the old and the new together.

The post-and-beam construction in this addition to the Baird residence allows for maximum window area and light penetration into the space. This living room, positioned at the end of a long series of "shotgun" rooms, not only gives a nice definition to the end but also provides ample borrowed light for the other rooms.

*All of the Bairds' furnishings were gathered from
flea markets, junk shops, and antiques stores.*

The Keaton Cabin

A small Montana cabin belonging to Michael Keaton was originally a homestead cabin built by Clarence Farnsworth in the
1920s. It wasn't his original homestead cabin but, rather, one he
built in anticipation of getting married. "He was hunting for a
bride," relates builder Terry Baird, "so he built himself a pretty
fancy little shack with hewn logs inside and out, dovetail corners,
and a little loft bedroom upstairs—a pretty classic little cabin."
Unfortunately, the bride never did materialize. For Keaton, the
cabin was moved to a new site and restacked. The roof was built
with the original log rafters, but a new dormer was added for the
second-floor loft.

The rear addition that houses the kitchen is made neither of logs
nor sheathed in log slabs. Rather, it is sided with antique boards
salvaged from an old calving shed. The ideally weathered boards
were applied vertically to the new frame addition and merge
seamlessly into the color and fabric of the building. Though it is
clearly an addition, the two pieces look as if they have been
connected for a hundred years.

Another interesting tidbit about this particular cabin is that much
of the furniture and cabinets were salvaged from the original
homestead cabin. A keen eye and a resourceful attitude allowed
for the interior as well as the exterior of this cottage to retain its
original character.

Though this kitchen is all new construction, it was
carefully crafted so as not to look "modern."

60

The dormers on the front of this cabin turned a cramped second floor into a much-more-useable bedroom space. The addition on the back is sheathed in boards salvaged from a calving shed.

Blending Tips

As an overall strategy for blending old and new, one needs to study and reflect on the type, color, texture, and proportions of the materials that exist in the building being reclaimed. An effort should be made to harmonize all repairs, renovations, alterations, or additions with those existing conditions.

The more old and reclaimed materials you can use, the easier it will be to integrate the old with the new. Often, a little extra work will be required to reuse old building parts, but you can sometimes make up for the time in reduced materials cost. Since most people are likely to be more adventuresome or playful when reclaiming a settler's cabin, they are also more willing to consider previously owned materials as utilitarian or artistic additions to their hideaway.

Architectural salvage is available almost everywhere. Most cities of any size have warehouses, or "emporiums," whose business it is to collect, sometimes refurbish, and resell salvaged materials. Chapters of Habitat for Humanity sometimes auction building materials to raise money for building affordable housing. Building contractors, and especially demolition contractors, are good sources. Keeping a keen eye on your neighborhood, on your county roads or city streets, can result in salvage opportunities. Sometimes owners are willing to sell, and sometimes they are just happy to give their "rubbish" to someone who is willing to haul it off. In keeping with the adage that one person's trash is another's treasure, even a landfill can produce bounty for the discriminating hunter—but be sure to check local regulations regarding wandering around a public landfill. Salvage is everywhere, you just have to tune your eyes and brain to see it.

Salvaged components that are most useful on homestead remodelings include windows, doors, plumbing fixtures, lighting fixtures, and hardware. Salvaged materials include roofing, woodwork, logs, boards, wood flooring, and stone. Almost anything that is not broken, rotted, or completely rusted out can be creatively reused for something—though not always for the purpose for which it was originally intended.

The more old and
reclaimed materials you
can use, the easier it
will be to integrate the
old with the new.

A word of caution: Rooting around in old or dismantled buildings has inherent dangers. Broken glass, rusty nails, rotting timbers, and hidden caches of old paint or insecticide present opportunities for accidents to occur. All of the standard safety procedures apply and should be followed. Here are a few, but no list could cover them all:

- *Wear goggles*

- *Wear gloves*

- *Don't lift objects that are too heavy for you*

- *Have an up-to-date tetanus shot*

- *Wear sturdy boots*

- *Make sure the electricity is OFF*

- *Remove nails from boards as you go*

- *Pay attention and use good common sense*

67

Left:
A skillful combination of recycled materials, along with a few new boards, resulted in an attractive front entrance to this barn/studio.

68

The pluses associated with using reclaimed components and materials are numerous. In addition to the obvious environmental issues, recycled ingredients can add interest and value, they can be (but are not always) cheaper, and they always stimulate good after-dinner stories and conversation. The drawbacks are the related unknowns, the fitting challenges, and the unreliable replacement resources that are inherent with salvage. Some items, because of their rarity, popularity, or designation by dealers as antiques, have gotten more expensive than comparable new ones. One can't always calculate the structural integrity or guarantee the exact ingredients of retrieved materials. If the Good Housekeeping Seal or USDA or FDA labels are important to you, salvage will probably make you nervous. Of course, as with all building materials you choose, you will need to make certain they comply with local building codes.

In any alteration or addition, new materials almost certainly will be required; you need to choose them carefully so that they will be in character with your existing building. It can absolutely wreck the appearance of an old cabin to wedge glitzy new materials designed for the new millennium against timeless materials intended for another era. For example, there is no faster way to destroy the vintage character of an old cabin than to put on a shiny, new, bright green or bright red metal roof. The roof may keep the foul weather out, but it won't convince the neighbors about your sense of good taste.

Ask yourself these questions when considering the purchase of new materials:

- *Does this material complement the original building components?*
- *Do the colors call attention to themselves? Do I want them to?*
- *Can I change the colors?*
- *If I choose to, can I hide this material? Where? How?*
- *Over time, will this material attain a natural patina that will be pleasing?*
- *Is there a way to artificially age this material? If I do that, will it deteriorate the product or void the warranty? Do I care?*
- *Is there a recycled material I could use that would be less expensive, more authentic, or more interesting?*
- *Have I considered all of the alternatives?*
- *Am I choosing this material because it is cheap, or because it is right for my project?*

This cabin beside a well-traveled roadway was made from logs salvaged from an old barn. The cabin was intentionally sited to be hidden from the view of passersby. Because it is set into the side of a hill, its rear wall is actually concrete.

Exterior Walls and Finishes

The palette of exterior wall materials for a recycled-cabin project includes logs, log slabs, wood siding, and stone.

If you are relocating an old cabin, it is very likely that you will need to replace a log or two due to rot, termite damage, or cuts and gashes that are beyond repair. Damaged logs can be removed and replaced with new, but be careful and particular about the new ones so that they have the best chance of matching the old. Find logs that are a comparable size, and make sure you work with deadfall or standing dead trees, not green wood. Unless you have the luxury of having such material on your property, you'll have to scout around a bit, but the material is available. With certain restrictions, you can even get a permit to remove dead logs from some state and federal lands. Please don't poach! Follow the rules so as to protect the environment.

If the logs in your old cabin are round, then you need only to
find a source of similar-sized ones to make repairs and additions.
If, however, the logs are hewn or were sawn with flat faces,
you'll need to find a way to get new logs sawn and sized to fit
your project. Depending on proximity, a sawmill could do the
work for you. There are also companies such as Wood-Mizer®
that manufacture portable sawmills starting at around $5,000
retail (see Resources, p. 129). If your job is not big enough to
justify a purchase, you could call the company to find out who
in your area owns one of these rigs. They might be willing to
rent one to you or to saw the logs you need.

If your cabin is hewn, don't try to build an addition with round
logs or finish the outside with half-round log slabs. It just won't
look like it belongs. Instead, build your addition from sawn logs,
hewn logs, or wood frame finished with horizontal or vertical
wood siding that is aged to match the color of your original logs.
(More about aging on p. 98.)

New "old" logs have been sawn on the Wood-Mizer®
and stacked in the construction of a cabin.

Most settlers' cabins were built with little or no underground footings and not much in the way of a foundation. Usually, a few stones were piled at the corners and other critical bearing points, but infrequently was a full foundation built. Local building codes as well as good building practices will dictate the proper footing and foundation for your reclaimed cabin and any additions you might make to it. And most building codes require some minimum crawl space for wiring, plumbing, and other utilities.

Building a true and level stone foundation can be costly and time consuming. As an alternative, you may want to consider adding a stone veneer to your cement or block foundation before or after you stack the logs. This will give your cabin a more rustic appearance and help to visually anchor it to the ground. Choose rocks carefully so that they are manageable in size and blend with the other natural conditions on your site. Usually, a local stone is preferable and less expensive. If you are inexperienced in choosing stone, it will be helpful to look at another foundation, building, or chimney that has been built of the same material before making your final decision.

This new log wall is secured together with large lag screws. The spaces between the logs will eventually be chinked.

Right: A dinner bell that may have sent out the "chow's on" message to family and hired hands working in the corrals provides interest, along with an antique lantern and an architectural detail, on the corner of this cabin.

Kitchens

In today's home, the kitchen has become one of the most important gathering places. In fact, in new home construction, kitchens are often larger than an entire homestead cabin would have been.

Since you are building a relatively unconventional project, it's important to think about your kitchen in a different way. Try considering the space as a collection of different cabinets, hutches, appliances, worktops, cutting areas, and storage places. You won't be able to buy this kitchen out of a catalog or at your local big-box home store. With some additional effort you can create a room with a sense of place and personality rather than another utilitarian kitchen where you go to prepare another meal.

Above: A standard refrigerator/freezer has been covered with wood paneling to fit the décor of the kitchenen.

This kitchen is a combination of freestanding cabinets and hutches along with built-in cabinets. The end result is the look of crafted furniture rather than standardized kitchen cabinets.

78

Rather than building uniform-sized and -shaped cabinets, think about building them out of different materials, in unique shapes, and with their purposes in mind. Perhaps you can find some old cabinets or hutches that can be incorporated into the design. Countertops don't have to be uniform in color or made of plastic laminate. Copper, galvanized steel, stainless steel, clay tile, stone, and butcher-block wood can be put to various uses, depending upon the functional requirements. Over time, copper and galvanized steel age and patinate beautifully. A new wood butcher-block surface gains character as it is used over the years—or perhaps you can find one that was already used somewhere else. Appliances like the refrigerator and dishwasher can have panels laminated to their surfaces so that they blend rather than shine in your kitchen.

An Acme kitchen that includes sink, stove, and cabinets in one steel unit makes this tiny guest cabin maximally functional.

A copper countertop complements these cabinets that have been finished with an aged-paint look.

Who would have thought that a century later we would want a kitchen like great-grandma's?

Some examples of old-style cabinets built of new wood.

Bathrooms

Since indoor plumbing is a relatively new development in this country, it's fair to say that homesteaders didn't wrestle with this issue. Making the bathroom fit the rustic nature of your home requires some extra effort. There are two major issues: fixtures and finishes.

When choosing fixtures, there are three choices: standard big-box-store units, renovated and recycled pieces, or new fixtures made to look old. Claw-foot bathtubs used to be tossed out and relegated to lives as plant holders or watering troughs. But in recent times they have become popular again, so, when you find one, it may be a bit expensive. Reproduction tubs like this are also available from a number of sources such as Renovator's Supply or Bathroom Machineries. Old sinks are a little easier to find. Check with plumbing contractors or architectural salvage yards. Before purchasing, make sure that the sink can be refitted with new faucets. And, of course, with any old fixture, make sure that it is not cracked and that it will hold water. Recycled toilets are a bit more of a challenge. Unless you have a way of knowing that one is still in good working order, it is probably best to choose something new. There are many styles of antique-reproduction toilets on the market. Alternatively, you can buy a standard model, put on a wooden seat, and call it good.

*This new bathroom cabinet is made to look old with
an aged-board finishing technique. Decorative tacks
are applied in an attractive pattern.*

82

A one-room guest cabin includes this antique reproduction sink and tub. The toilet is in a private compartment.

84

When you think about finishes for the bathroom, consider some alternatives to the normal ceramic-tile walls, plastic vanity tops, and vinyl-tile floors. Properly finished wood floors will wear and last as long as any tile floor you can buy. Shower surrounds can be built of a combination of wood, glass, and tile, and vanity tops can be covered with copper or galvanized metal as a rustic alternative. As with the kitchen, the bathroom can be a collection of hutches and freestanding cabinets. Try making the bathroom a place to "be" instead of just a place to "go."

Of course, if your cabin is in a remote location, an outdoor privy or a composting toilet might be the authentic solution. In most places, privies are still allowed as long as they are constructed according to certain health standards. Composting toilets allow you to avoid digging a drain field if you don't have indoor access to water or if your property doesn't properly perk for a septic field.

A fancy log outhouse.

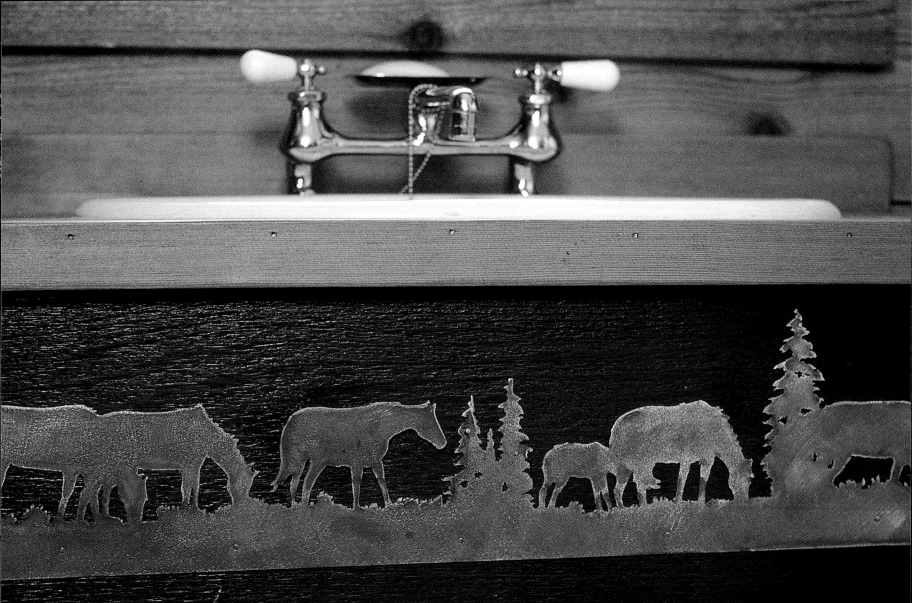

Showering outdoors in this wood facility is a necessity at the small cabin where it is located—but what an invigorating experience!

*Unique shower doors and the vanity are all made
to look old. The vanity features a galvanized
metal top and a recycled sink.*

Electricity

Another issue homesteaders did not have to face was how to hide electrical wires. Given the probability that you will want electricity in your cabin, you should plan in advance not only where you want lights and receptacles but how to get power to them without having to staple exposed wire to the walls. Most areas require, by law, that electrical work be done by a licensed professional. Unless you find someone who specializes in working with old log buildings, you'll want to personally supervise this part of the work closely so that the wiring is done in a way that is sympathetic to the restoration. Wires can be run beneath the floor, behind chinking joints in logs, along the base log and covered by molding, and behind door or window casings. In some instances, logs might need to be drilled to get wires just where you want them. This implies, of course, that you have some sort of wiring layout to work from before you start the work. It can always be modified, but thinking about these things in advance will save time and money in the process. This is more easily done while the logs are being stacked than after they are in place.

Steve Aller turned standard reproduction push-button wall switches into miniature pieces of art with a custom steel cover plate.

*A custom electric wall sconce in the
style of Thomas Molesworth adds a
soft glow to this cozy cabin room.*

90

Light fixtures are also an important consideration. Recessed cans and fluorescent ceiling fixtures don't really have a place in a reclaimed settler's cabin. There are a number of manufacturers, such as Rejuvenation Lamp & Fixture Company (see Resources, p. 129), that make reproduction period light fixtures. Also, consider receptacles that are switched at the wall to turn on lamps instead of a ceiling light.

Think of wiring and lighting as a big puzzle, with the winning solution being that all wiring is safely concealed at the completion of the job with few or no extension cords required.

Above: Reproduction antique overhead lights are a classy fit for this richly furnished cabin.
Right: An authentic kerosene lantern has been retrofitted with electricity and claims an honored place on an exterior wall as a beacon of welcome.

Tips, Tricks, and Concoctions

The following recipes are a result of experimentation, over time, with many products on many projects. There is no exact formula for any of them, so the results are not completely predictable. These recipes have worked—but many more attempts have failed. Half the fun is in the trying, so experiment, don't be intimidated by failure, and allow yourself to be surprised. As with any natural aging process, breaking down some of the intrinsic or artificial protection of the materials lessens the life of the product. If it is important to you that things last forever and look shiny and new, this is probably not information you will want to apply to your building process.

Weathered boards and rusty hinges, whether reclaimed or created, are a must for the homestead-cabin look.

*Imagine how inconsistent a shiny galvanized-
metal roof would look over these weathered logs.*

Aging Natural Wood

Unless they have been painted (heaven forbid—get out the sand-blaster!), old log buildings have weathered over time to a wonderful shade of soft gray. The Japanese have a word—*sabi*—that attaches aesthetic value to such things. As you replace rotted logs or add additions made of newly sawn logs or rough-sawn boards, one of the blending challenges is to get the new wood to look like it has been a part of the building for many years. Time will solve the problem if you want to wait twenty years. But if you can't wait, an inexpensive magic potion will speed the aging process from years to hours.

Ferrous sulfate is a chemical that is used to fertilize golf courses, in water treatment plants, and, in a slightly different form, as an iron supplement to enrich flour (as in store-bought bread). A lawn-and-garden-supply or farm-and-ranch store should have it.

Mix a handful of the ferrous sulfate thoroughly with five gallons of water. Strain the liquid through some cheesecloth or fine-screen wire and pour it into a standard garden sprayer. (It is probably a good idea to buy an inexpensive sprayer that will be used only for this purpose.) Then, simply spray this mixture onto new wood logs or boards. In a very short time, they will begin to turn gray. Some wood may show a slight green cast for a while, but that will disappear over time. Wood with open grain (rough sawn) will turn gray more readily than wood with a really tight grain. When using new wood, leave it stacked outside for a while before using it and the grain will begin to open up, making the wood age a little more readily. As with any other applied finishes, experiment with some scraps before you spray the entire front of your new home. Also, be sure to take the same reasonable precautions that you would when spraying any other paint, fertilizer, or garden chemical: wear a mask, goggles, and gloves while you work.

A ferrous sulfate solution turned the new fir boards gray for a weathered-looking porch floor.

Rusting Hinges and Hardware

Old cabins don't have bright new hardware. New galvanized hinges and hardware can be rusted and made to look old by dipping them for a short period of time into a plastic pan or bowl partially filled with muriatic acid. This will strip off the galvanizing and allow the metal to rust. The thinner the metal, the less time it need remain in the acid. If you leave it too long, the metal will completely dissolve. After taking the hardware out of the acid, wash it thoroughly in water and leave it outdoors to begin the rusting process. If you live in a climate with low humidity, it will help to mist the hardware and leave it under a moist rag or towel. When the material looks like you want it to, buff it slightly with steel wool; depending upon how you are going to use it, you may wish to preserve the finish with some spray lacquer or paste wax.

An alternative to this artificial rusting process is to find old hinges and hardware that have already rusted naturally and to use those instead of new ones.

Be extremely careful with muriatic acid as it is highly toxic and will burn. Wear gloves and eye protection; work in a ventilated area—preferably outside. Take all necessary precautions not to breathe the fumes and to carefully follow the manufacturer's directions provided on the product container.

Another method for accomplishing the same kind of rusting process is to dip the hardware in a full-strength bath of vinegar. Since vinegar is a much weaker acid, the process will take longer but is a lot safer and won't require such strict safety precautions. Even with vinegar, never mix metal and an acid in a closed container. The expanding gasses will cause the container to burst.

These hinges, rescued from a pile of junk, make interesting and useful brackets to join a roof beam and a column.

The Japanese call it sabi, the venerable patina of age that aesthetically anchors an object to its natural surroundings.

Aging Painted-Wood Finishes

If you have found an old piece of furniture, it is highly likely that it has been painted more than once with more than one color. There are dents and blemishes on the wood, and the edges are probably worn and smooth.

To make a new piece of wood look old, go over it first with the flame from a propane torch to open the grain. Burning it slightly won't hurt. It can be sanded back, and some of the burn marks will add character to the finish. Next, thin some latex paint a bit with water (two parts water to one part paint) and wash it over a rough-sawn board. After it has dried, go over the surface with an orbital sander; this will smooth the board somewhat and remove some of the paint. If you like what you see, leave it alone. If it needs a bit more paint, repeat the process, perhaps with a different color. After you get the color just like you want it, the piece can be finished with a finishing oil or paste wax.

When building furniture with old boards, take time to fill nail holes with wood putty. And whether you're working with old boards or new boards made to look like old, use rusty nails so that you won't have any "shiners" showing through.

New wood finished with an aged-wood tech-
nique resulted in some fine kitchen cabinets.
The simple wood latch adds to a vintage look.

Miscellaneous Tips

- *When using old boards, new wood will appear when you make a saw cut. Burn the new surface with a torch until it turns black. This will open the grain and change the texture of the wood. Sand it back and then mist the board with a spray paint—white, flat black, or gray. Don't use a heavy coat. Sand again and the newly cut end should look old. If it doesn't, repeat the process.*

- *Shiny galvanized roofing can be washed down with a weakened solution of muriatic acid, then rinsed with water and sprayed with a ferrous sulfate solution to take off the sheen. This will, of course, take some of the life out of the roof, so make this decision carefully and employ safety precautions when using an acid wash. If you decide to do this, or to use old rusty tin that you have salvaged, your sub roof needs to be the layer that actually keeps out the water. There are many excellent products on the market today for this purpose. The metal roofing then acts as physical protection for the sub roof.*

- *Copper screens in new windows will age rather quickly and will last a long time.*

- *Any new wood left outside, unprotected, will begin to age. If you have plenty of time before you need the material, it can be stacked outside to let the elements do the aging work.*

- *A little cement mixed with water will turn redwood dark gray or black almost instantly.*

- *A large handful of rusty nails left in a bucket of water will make a wash that can be used to age boards.*

HOUSE INTO HOME

In the beginning, a reclaimed homestead cabin is usually a simple, unadorned structure without a lot of sizzle, pop, and flash. In order to gain enough space for daily living, one might add some "saddlebags" here and there, paste on a porch or two, or blend two or three buildings together as one. The initial basic rectangular form may be changed somewhat, but if you are successful in retaining the homestead aesthetic, when your home is complete you will still have only a series of boxes stacked together in a pleasing composition.

What, then, transfigures these unadorned logs and old boards into spaces filled with exuberance, giving each space—inside and out—a sense of adventure and delight? It's all in the selection of materials, finishes, colors, furniture, and even the really small things like light-switch covers and towel bars. Some may call this activity "decorating," but it's really more than that. Paying attention to all of the details throughout the entire construction process is what makes the distinction between simply occupying a habitable space and the complex synergy of melding with the atmosphere of a warm and enchanting abode.

From paints and finishes to gates and latches; from furniture, art, and artifacts to floor materials and coverings—all of the parts and pieces are ingredients to the recipe for success. The following photographs may give you some ideas and inspiration as you begin this very important journey of transforming your cabin from house into home.

*A unique outdoor sink made of wood is a
clever detail, blending well with the old
boards on this cabin addition.*

All of the parts and pieces are ingredients to the recipe for success.

The pole railing merges into the aspen trees,
which provide a backdrop for antique dippers.

The recycled wire gate hung on wood posts with an overhead brace defines the entry point and adds interest to an old fence.

Rusted-metal silhouettes affixed to the cabinet and mirror frame pull together the color scheme of this bathroom.

*A new handcrafted screen door has been made to look old by the
application of a graying compound on the surface of the wood,
copper screen, and custom wood detailing at the corners.*

Two porch lights here, instead of one, enhance the balanced symmetry of the cabin's facade.

An antique dinner bell seems authentic on these log ends.

One doesn't always have to make the obvious choice
when working with natural materials. Instead of a single
porch post, this shed roof is held up with a column that
begins as a single tree but branches out to two in the
middle. You won't find such columns in the wood store,
but you can usually find them in the woods.

Someone with a sharp eye for reusable junk rescued this
well-worn light fixture whose patina is perfectly matched
to the weathered porch rafters.

112

Old kerosene lanterns can be "electrified" and used
as exterior light fixtures. If you decide to use these
kinds of lights, make sure they comply with your
local electrical code requirements.

Another venerable lighting fixture
rescued for a new life.

Corners provide marvelous
opportunities for enhancing
a cabin with artistic details.

Steve Aller's steel artistry adds interest and definition to this
porch-rafter corner. Copper window screens partner attrac-
tively with the log construction.

Stone is a most-companionable foundation for aged timber or log walls.

This stone building base was laid by amateur masons. They took care to make sure there were no "lightning bolts"—joints you can trace from the top to the bottom of the wall.

*Carefully planned details come together
in rich artistic expression.*

In addition to providing protection from the weather, this small back porch helps define the entry and affords an outdoor space for reading or napping.

Floor boards laid at perpendicular angles create an interesting detail at the corner of this wraparound porch.

Authentically vintage or made to look vintage? Who can tell? The ensemble works confidently on a glassed-in porch.

Color, art, light—perfect details for a per-
fectly cozy nest for reading or napping.

An exterior door is recycled for new use as a bathroom
door. The original glass has been replaced with etched
glass that adds interest and assures privacy.

Picture-perfect: precise dovetail joinery and
a few well-placed hooks for fishing gear.
This is what turns a house into a home.

122

*Whitewash on this dormer increases the
apparent size of interior space, acts as a
light "scoop," and provides an ideal
light source for this antique desk.*

*Built-in beds with their own stor-
age drawers below convert the space
under the low end of a shed roof
into a generous bunkhouse.*

Geometrics in the architecture and the bed covers speak volumes in this tiny space.

This old door has seen
many comings and goings.
Now, as a part of a newly
recycled building, it has a
chance to say "welcome" to
a different set of travelers.

RESOURCES

Books and Magazines

American Country: The Country Kitchen. New York:
Time-Life Books, 1988.

• Great photographs of country kitchens. This is part of an old
Time-Life book series; it is not in print anymore but can be
found in used-book stores or in one of the used-book search
engines on the Web, such as www.bibliofind.com.

Burns, Max. *Cottage Water Systems.* Toronto, Ontario: Cottage
Life Books, 1995.

• A complete guide to cabin water systems, including water
sources, pumps, plumbing, septic systems, and outhouses.

Drinkard, G. Lawson, III. *Retreats: Handmade Hideaways to
Refresh the Spirit.* Salt Lake City: Gibbs Smith, Publisher, 1997.
• An essential resource for anyone dreaming about a personal retreat.

Ewald, Chase Reynolds. *Cowboy Chic,* Salt Lake City: Gibbs
Smith, Publisher, 2000.

• Spotlighting artisans and homes that represent the newest
western décor but celebrate both the region and its traditions.

Hunt, W. Ben. *How to Build and Furnish a Log Cabin.*
New York: Macmillan Publishing Company, 1974.

• Originally published in 1939 and 1947, this book is a guide to
building cabins and furniture with hand tools in the pioneer style.

Innes, Jocasta. *The New Paint Magic.* New York:
Pantheon Books, 1992.

• A complete guide to painted finishes on walls,
woodwork, floors, and furniture.

Kylloe, Ralph. *Cabin Collectibles.* Salt Lake City:
Gibbs Smith, Publisher, 2000.

• The insider's guide to the best antique cabin collectibles.

————. *Rustic Artistry for the Home.* Gibbs Smith,
Publisher, 2000.

• The most talented new rustic-furniture artists, along with
regional styles and past masters, are presented here.

McRaven, Charles. *Building and Restoring the Hewn Log House.*
Cincinnati, Ohio: Betterway Books, 1994.

• Step-by-step instructions to restore or build a
hewn-log house.

————. *Building with Stone.* Pownal, Vermont: Storey
Communications, Inc. (A Garden Way Publishers Book), 1989.

• An introduction to the philosophy, art, and craft of stone
construction. Lots of practical information and pointers on
selecting stone and on building dams, bridges, fireplaces, barns,
and houses.

Manning, Richard. *A Good House*. New York:
Penguin Books USA, 1993.

• Manning's story of designing and constructing his own
timber-frame house near Missoula is filled with practical and
philosophical advice about everything from environmental
issues to financing to alternative toilets.

Mother Earth News

• A bimonthly magazine full of articles that range from bale
houses, to single-person hot tubs, to natural gardening tips,
as well as a source for purchasing retreat-related products
and books.

Old House Journal Restoration Directory

• An annual publication of leading products for restoration
and renovation enthusiasts. For more information, call
800-234-3797 and log-on to www.oldhousejournal.com.

Ruoff, Abby, with photography by Michael Watson.
Rustic Country: Handmade Accents for the Home.
Salt Lake City: Gibbs Smith, Publisher, 2000.

• Guidelines for creating handmade accents for the home
  from natural materials.

Taylor, Stephen. *Building Thoreau's Cabin*. Wainscott,
New York: Pushcart Press, 1992.

• Some philosophy and lots of practical guidance for building
a simple personal cabin space at an affordable price.

Teipner-Thiede, Cindy, and Arthur Thiede. *The Log Home
Book: Design, Past and Present*. Salt Lake City: Gibbs Smith,
Publisher, 1993.

• Lessons and legacies from the architectural past, with fresh
ideas for building a modern log home.

Thiede, Cindy and Arthur. *Hands-on Log Homes*. Salt Lake City:
Gibbs Smith, Publisher, 1998.

• Includes information on owner-built homes, recycled log
homes, and historical restorations.

Tillotson, Betty. *Skills for Simple Living*. Point Roberts,
Washington: Hartley & Marks, Inc., 1991.

• Practical ideas, from outdoor clay ovens to simple solar
hot-water systems; from gourd mandolins to bay-leaf bug repellent.

Traditional Building Magazine

• A bimonthly magazine of articles, product information, and
sources for traditional building products. See the Web site at
www.traditional-building.com

White, Linda. *Log Spirit*. Salt Lake City: Gibbs Smith, Publisher,
2000.

• Ten details that can turn any house into a cozy cabin.

Wick, William S. *Log Cabins and Cottages: How to Build and Furnish Them.* Salt Lake City: Gibbs Smith, Publisher, 1999.

• Originally printed more than a half century ago, this little book captures the spirit of the resurgence of man's interest in rustic traditions.

 Equipment, Tools, Furniture, Other Good Stuff & People

Steve Aller
Boulder River Ranch, McLeod, MT 59052, 406-932-6406

• Custom steel cutouts, original ranch signs, and cowboy cartoons.

T. Baird Construction
Box 1, McLeod, MT 59052, 406-932-6116

• Custom-built homes and retreats from used logs, adapted structures, and salvaged materials. Also new, if that's what you really want.

Bathroom Machineries
495 Main Street, Murphys, CA 95247, 800-255-4426

• Catalog of antique plumbing fixtures, hard-to-find parts, and decorator accessories.

Chuck Wagon Outfitters
250 Avila Beach Drive, San Luis Obispo, CA 93405, 800-543-2359

• Cast-iron cookware, lanterns, books, and accessories.

Diane Cole-Ross Rustic Furniture
10 Cloninger Lane, Bozeman, MT 59715, 406-587-3373

• One-of-a-kind custom willow and lodgepole furniture.

Conklin's Authentic Antique Barnwood & Hand Hewn Beams
RD #1 Box 70, Susquehanna, PA 18847, 717-465-3832
Web site: www.conklinsbarnwood.com

• Reclaimed vintage lumber.

Cumberland General Store
Route 3, Crossville, TN 38555, 800-334-4640

• Lamps, lanterns, fireplace accessories, blacksmith's tools, windmills, hand pumps, porch swings, violin kits, quilting frames, cider presses, country kitchen utensils, and just about everything else.

Audrey S. Hall, Photographer
121 North Yellowstone, Livingston, MT 59047, 406-222-2450

• Photographs of your retreat or for your brochure.

Lehman's Non-Electric Catalog
P.O. Box 41, Kidron, OH 44636, 216-857-5757

• Non-electric lighting, non-electric appliances, cookstoves, woodstoves, and composting toilets.

Mountain Lumber
P.O. Box 289, Ruckersville, VA 22968, 800-445-2671
Web site: www.mountainlumber.com

• Reclaimed antique lumber.

Plow and Hearth
P.O. Box 5000, Madison, VA 22727, 800-627-1712
Web site: www.plowhearth.net

• Furnishings and decorations for country living.

Real Goods
800-762-7325 toll-free, 715-824-5021 fax
Web site: www.realgoods.com

• Woodstoves, cookstoves, hearth products, solar thermal systems, composting toilets, renewable-energy products.

Rejuvenation Lamp & Fixture Company
2550 NW Nicolai Street, Portland, OR 97210, 888-343-8548
Web site: www.rejuvenation.com

• Authentic re-created lamps and light fixtures.

Simpson Gallagher Gallery
1115 - 13th Street, Cody, WY 82414, 307-587-4022

• Western paintings, prints, sculpture, and other items of delight and culture for your cabin.

Wood-Mizer®
8180 West 10th Street, Indianapolis, IN 46214, 800-553-0182
Web site: www.woodmizer.com

• Portable personal sawmills; demo video available.

Woodworkers Supply
800-645-9292 toll-free

• A great source for tools of all types.